30 DAYS

THROUGH A

CRISIS

30 DAYS

THROUGH A

CRISIS

DAILY DEVOTIONS TO NAVIGATE YOUR FAITH

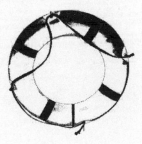

DR. ABIDAN SHAH, PHD
& NICOLE SHAH

DEDICATION

This devotional is dedicated to our Clearview Church
family.

"We give thanks to the God and Father of our Lord Jesus
Christ, praying always for you"

Colossians 1:3

CONTENTS

INTRODUCTION

"I've never seen anything like this in all my life…and I've lived through a lot!"

A senior adult friend of mine greeted me with those words. Of course, he was referring to the current nationwide shutdown due to the Coronavirus (COVID-19) crisis. Even though I haven't lived as long as this person, I couldn't agree more. It feels like every day, we are trudging deeper and deeper into a murky dream (more like a nightmare) and, at any moment, we'll all wake up to normalcy.

Unfortunately, it's very real and we're all wide awake. Right before our eyes, schools and college campuses are closed; more and more businesses have shut down, some for the very last time; restaurants are unable to stay open and keep paying their employees; working class people in America are worried about their jobs and some now have zero income; and travels and vacations have all been cancelled. People are scared to go anywhere, and most places are closed down anyway. The list continues. There is no denying that we are in an unprecedented crisis.

How do we respond to all this commotion? Do we hunker down and wait for the worst to pass? Do we stick our heads in the sand and pretend that everything is fine? As Nicole and I pondered all of this, we felt that we needed to prayerfully help those around us navigate through these uncharted waters. Everyone has been affected one way or another from this crisis. People are searching for answers and, sadly, many are coming up fearful and hopeless.

Nicole and I have found ourselves in similar places before and it felt horrible. We prayed that God would show us how we can shine His light in these dark days.

The idea of the 30-day devotional through crisis came to us as we went out on our weekly date. So much had changed in the past couple of weeks. It was lunch time, but the roads were empty and seemed to stretch farther than we remembered. Shops and businesses everywhere were closed, lining the streets like tombstones. It was incredibly eerie. We asked ourselves, "What is it that we would like to be reminded of at a time like this?" One by one, certain words came to our mind that became the chapter headings for our 30-day devotional. Our prayer is that this little book will not only help you now but far outlive this crisis and even help future readers during whatever crises that may come in their lives.

Thanks are due to the Clearview team! They each took on a specific role that they were most qualified to do— Rebecca Shah (editor), Ryan Hill (design and layout), John Galantis (creative insights), and David Williamson and Kelsey McKeel (final edits). This project would not have been successful without their help (and their families too). Of course, we are responsible for any mistakes in this work. We are especially grateful to our Clearview Church family. It is such a joy to know that our leaders are always behind us no matter the circumstances. Finally, we are grateful to our kids—Rebecca, Abigail, Nicholas, and Thomas—for serving alongside without a single complaint (other than an occasional "we're hungry" from the boys).

As you walk through this book over the next 30 days, just know that we are praying for everyone who picks up this book. Our prayer is that while you face this crisis, God will guide and strengthen you through His Word into the image of His Son by the Holy Spirit.

1. DAILY DEVOTIONS

Crises disrupt the equilibrium of our lives. They cause us to doubt and question the truth about God and His Word. It is vital that we maintain a strong devotional life during tough times. Unfortunately, this is often the first thing to go out the window. It's understandable, but the sooner we can get back to daily Bible reading and prayer, the better.

The Bible is God's Word for us and it's the only source of absolute truth we'll ever find. Every day, we have a choice either to fill our minds with fear and doubt or with the promises and principles of God. If we choose the latter, it will help us combat the lies that the Enemy whispers in our ears during times of crisis. You will be amazed at how much of what you read in your quiet time will come back to you when you need it the most.

If reading the Scriptures is how God speaks to you, then prayer is your opportunity to speak to God. Of course, God doesn't have to be informed regarding what's happening. He already knows every struggle you'll ever encounter. And yet, He wants us to tell Him about our circumstances and ask Him for our needs.

During His time on earth, even Jesus, the Son of God and the second Person of the Godhead, would rise up long before daylight and go off to a secluded place to pray. How much more do we need to do the same? James reminds us "you do not have because you do not ask" (James 4:2d). Not only that, but let us continue to stay in a spirit of prayer.

Every moment, every step, and every decision we make during a crisis should be approached with prayer.

<u>Scriptures to Think On:</u>

Your word is a lamp to my feet and a light to my path. **Psalm 119:105**

This Book of the Law shall not depart from your mouth, but you shall meditate in it day and night, that you may observe to do according to all that is written in it. For then you will make your way prosperous, and then you will have good success. **Joshua 1:8**

Be anxious for nothing, but in everything by prayer and supplication, with thanksgiving, let your requests be made known to God. **Philippians 4:6**

Then He (Jesus) spoke a parable to them, that men always ought to pray and not lose heart. **Luke 18:1**

JOURNAL

_____

_____

_____

_____

_____

_____

_____

_____

_____

_____

_____

_____

_____

_____

2. GRACE

Life can be unfair, especially during times of crisis. We question God—"Why are we suffering? Why aren't You coming to our rescue?" What's worse, we see others going about their daily lives with little to no trouble and wonder why they have it so easy. But the root cause is more than just envy or a desire for fairness. Ultimately, we doubt God's justice. In times like these, we need God's amazing grace and His unmerited favor in our undeserving lives.

How do we recognize this grace? Sometimes, it comes to us like a single ray of sunshine breaking through the clouds on a dark and stormy day. Other times, it comes as an answer to prayers that we have been praying for a very long time. Still, there are those times when we sense the presence of God in a special way, like a quiet whisper in the middle of the whirlwind. These glimpses of God's grace come to us at the right time and in the right measure to lift us higher.

How do we get more of God's grace? The secret to maximum grace is maximum weakness. A perfect example is the Apostle Paul who suffered a thorn in his flesh to keep him humble. He prayed many times that it would leave him but the answer came back, "My grace is sufficient for you, for My strength is made perfect in weakness." So, Paul exclaimed, "Therefore most gladly I will rather boast in my infirmities, that the power of Christ may rest upon me. Therefore, I take pleasure in infirmities, in reproaches, in needs, in persecutions, in distresses, for Christ's sake. For when I am weak, then I am strong" (2 Corinthians 12:9b-10). Suffering and weakness are God's opportunities to release His grace into our lives.

Salvation is by grace through faith alone. If God's grace has brought us to where we are today, His grace will bring us through crises. And remember, grace is not a finite gift, but is new every day! If we are truly saved, the Bible says we are children of God. And as His children, we should be able to pinpoint different instances of God's grace in our lives. Try making a list of all the different ways that God has blessed you and be specific! This exercise will not only get our focus off of our circumstances, but get our focus on God's blessings and how He could be using a crisis to pour out even more grace in the lives of His children.

Scriptures to Think On:

So the LORD said, 'I will destroy man whom I have created from the face of the earth, both man and beast, creeping thing and birds of the air, for I am sorry that I have made them.' But Noah found grace in the eyes of the LORD. **Genesis 6:7-8**

But by the grace of God I am what I am, and His grace toward me was not in vain; but I labored more abundantly than they all, yet not I, but the grace of God which was with me. **1 Corinthians 15:10**

JOURNAL

_____

_____

_____

_____

_____

_____

_____

_____

_____

_____

_____

_____

_____

3. LOVE

Love is fragile. The slightest bump in our lives can greatly impact our capacity to show love to others. As a result, crises can make us appear unloving. This often gets misdiagnosed as being hateful, but that's not true. The actual culprit is fear. When fear begins to rule our hearts, it inhibits our ability to show love. Fortunately, love is also the only weapon that can drive out fear. Listen to what John says in 1 John 4:18: "There is no fear in love; but perfect love casts out fear, because fear involves torment. But he who fears has not been made perfect in love."

Fear causes us to doubt everything and suspect everyone. There is, of course, a place for healthy fear that makes us cautious and aware of our surroundings. However, it is impossible for us to show love when our hearts are full of fear. Think about the women who came to the tomb of Jesus on Easter morning. They were facing a terrible crisis: their Savior had been brutally crucified right before their eyes! But on the third day, their love for Jesus overcame their fear and brought them to the empty tomb where they became the first heralds of His resurrection. And where were His fearless disciples? They were hiding behind closed doors because their hearts were ruled by terror, not love.

How can we let love overcome fear in our lives, especially during difficult times? First, we have to understand the depth of God's love for us. There is no better way to discover the fullness of God's love than to look to the cross. Paul reminds us in Romans 5:8: "But God demonstrates His own love toward us, in that while we were still sinners, Christ died for us." Second, we have to let God fill us with His love until it begins to overflow in how we love others. John 15:12, "This is My commandment, that you love one another as I have loved you."

Begin praying and asking God to show you how to love people the way He loves us. As Nicole's father would often say, "Most people have never been loved properly." You will be amazed at the opportunities that God will orchestrate in your life as a result of those prayers. Capitalize on them and allow yourself to be a wellspring of God's love to others, driving out your own fears in the process.

Scriptures to Think On:

The LORD has appeared of old to me, saying: "Yes, I have loved you with an everlasting love; therefore, with lovingkindness I have drawn you. **Jeremiah 31:3**

Love suffers long and is kind; love does not envy; love does not parade itself, is not puffed up; does not behave rudely, does not seek its own, is not provoked, thinks no evil; does not rejoice in iniquity, but rejoices in the truth; bears all things, believes all things, hopes all things, endures all things. Love never fails….And now abide faith, hope, love, these three; but the greatest of these is love.
1 Corinthians 13:4-8a, 13

JOURNAL

4. PEACE

It's easy for us to confuse "peace" with "quiet." But peace is much more than just the absence of turmoil. It's the calm assurance that all is well and will turn out for the best.

Unfortunately, crisis has a way of destroying this assurance. Sometimes, it comes as a tidal wave that slams into our lives, leaving us drowning and gasping for air. Other times, it's a slow leak, invisible at first, but eventually depleting us of every ounce of peace, until all that's left is anxiety, stress, fear, and doubt. This was never the life God intended for His children!

So, how can we restore peace to our lives in the midst of a crisis? We should learn from the disciples who were caught in a storm on the Sea of Galilee. Now, keep in mind that these men were expert fishermen who had navigated the Sea of Galilee hundreds of times. They even knew that the lake was susceptible to sudden storms.

But for some reason, this storm was different. It was getting worse and worse, and they were about to sink! Just then, it hit the disciples that Jesus was with them! But where was He? He was in the stern, asleep on a pillow…" Listen to how they addressed Him in Mark 4:38, "And they awoke Him and said to Him, 'Teacher, do You not care that we are perishing?'" Their question is very revealing. They doubted His care for their lives. Peace evaporates when we doubt God's care for us.

But Jesus' response is equally revealing in verses 39-40, "Then He arose and rebuked the wind, and said to the sea, 'Peace, be still!' And the wind ceased and there was a great calm. But He said to them, 'Why are you so fearful? How is it that you have no faith?'" This means that our peace is directly connected to our faith.

Jesus is the Prince of Peace. He will grant His peace to us in abundance, but we have to surrender our fears and anxieties to Him. Peace and fear cannot occupy our minds at the same time. One will always win out over the other. Let us allow God to fill us with His peace that surpasses all understanding and watch as fear fades into the background of our minds. We need to trust Him that He is more than able to handle our crises and He will do as He has promised.

Scriptures to Think On:

You will keep him in perfect peace, whose mind is stayed on You, because he trusts in You.   **Isaiah 26:3**

Peace I leave with you, My peace I give to you; not as the world gives do I give to you. Let not your heart be troubled, neither let it be afraid.   **John 14:27**

Casting all your care upon Him, for He cares for you.
1 Peter 5:7

JOURNAL

_____

_____

_____

_____

_____

_____

_____

_____

_____

_____

_____

_____

_____

_____

5. WISDOM

Acquired knowledge, personal experiences, and a good dose of common sense...all of these can be helpful tools during a crisis. However, they are no substitute for godly wisdom. Knowledge helps us understand the inner workings of our problems. Our experiences give us a heads-up so we know what to expect. Common sense also helps us avoid making dumb decisions, but only godly wisdom can bring us into God's purpose and power.

When we go through a crisis, our natural tendency is to look for ways to escape. We may even go a step further, considering ways we can make the most of the problem and come out on top. But godly wisdom elevates us to where God is so that we can see what He is doing with the problem and submit to His plan. True wisdom doesn't look for a way out, but instead focuses on the heart of God and His purpose in every difficult moment.

Solomon claims in Proverbs 9:10, "The fear of the LORD is the beginning of wisdom, and the knowledge of the Holy One is understanding." In other words, godly wisdom comes only to those who fear God and desire to obey Him. He gives His wisdom only to those who ask in every situation, "What is God doing?" and "What does God want me to do?" If we listen to His wisdom, we will stand behind God and follow His directions through the crisis.

Of course, the Bible is full of godly wisdom, but let us not stop there. Let us go to the author of wisdom, who is wisdom personified: Jesus Christ, the Son of God. As Scriptures tell us, He is "Christ the power of God and the wisdom of God" (1 Corinthians 1:24). In Him "are hidden all the treasures of wisdom and knowledge" (Colossians 2:3). Have you asked Christ to be your wisdom through your crisis?

Scriptures to Think On:

When the whirlwind passes by, the wicked is no more, But the righteous (wise) has an everlasting foundation. **Proverbs 10:25**

If any of you lacks wisdom, let him ask of God, who gives to all liberally and without reproach, and it will be given to him. **James 1:5**

JOURNAL

_____

_____

_____

_____

_____

_____

_____

_____

_____

_____

_____

_____

_____

6. THANKFULNESS

During a crisis, we tend to lose sight of all the good we have and only focus on the difficulties we are experiencing. The Enemy uses this as an opportunity to wreak havoc in our minds. If we're not careful, our hearts can easily become bitter and discouraged. So many unnecessary conflicts and harsh words can be traced back to an ungrateful heart. The perfect antidote is a spirit of thankfulness.

But how do we do that in the midst of a crisis? Sometimes, it's tempting to give into the doom-and-gloom and ask, "How do I show gratefulness in all of this?" In these times of uncertainty, it's important to reflect on God's blessings in our lives.

Begin by thanking God for His daily blessings that we take for granted: health, family, shelter, food, vehicles, work, church family, our nation, etc. Next, reflect on His past blessings in our lives. Even though things may seem like a mess right now, hasn't God been faithful to us through the years? Can we not see His marvelous hand, guiding and blessing us through all of our circumstances?

Finally, let us not forget the spiritual blessings He gives to us. If we are honest, these blessings are far more valuable to us and they will outlast our crisis and every one to come! Here are just a few blessings that we can thank Him for: forgiveness of our sins through Jesus, the peace of God in our hearts, joy that is not dependent on our circumstances, mercies that are new every day, and hope that extends beyond the grave.

We may not be able to control the situation that we find ourselves in right now, but we can control how we choose to view them – through the eyes of thankfulness.

Scriptures to Think On:

Oh, give thanks to the LORD, for He is good! For His mercy endures forever. **Psalm 118:1**

Because, although they knew God, they did not glorify Him as God, nor were they thankful, but became futile in their thoughts, and their foolish hearts were darkened. **Romans 1:21**

In everything give thanks; for this is the will of God in Christ Jesus for you. **1 Thessalonians 5:18**

JOURNAL

---

7. HOPE

We all have a vision of how we want our lives to play out—blue skies, green grass, no troubles in sight. But all the same, those storm clouds roll in, darkening the sky and blotting out the sun for days on end. The twinkling stars we once loved vanish into a cold, black void. When everything is dark, it's difficult to see the end of our suffering. This is the same despair that POWs face when days become weeks and weeks become months and months become years with no hope of being free in sight. To lose hope is dangerous.

In times like these, we need that one ray of sunshine, that one star in the sky to remind us that everything will be okay. We need hope.

But, what does that word "hope" mean? It is so often misunderstood. Some use it as a desire for a positive outcome in the future: "I hope Santa brings me a new bike" or "I hope I find love one day." Others use it with a negative fear in mind: "I hope we make it on time" or "I've lost all hope."

But the biblical idea of hope is something very different. Biblical hope is the solid assurance that God already has something beautiful prepared for us in the future and that we will receive it without fail. If we seek hope on this side alone, we will always be disappointed. This world—full of pain, sickness, death and sorrow—is not our home, if we are born-again believers. Our permanent home is Heaven, where there will be no more tears, sorrow, pain or death. As

Hebrews 13:14 reminds us, "For here we have no continuing city, but we seek the one to come." Let us surrender our doubts to God today and let the Holy Spirit bring us this true lasting hope.

Even when the world around us might feel like it's unraveling, the hope that comes from a relationship with Jesus Christ defies our deepest fears. In His earthly ministry, everywhere Jesus went, He brought hope to people. He was and still is the Great Hope-Bringer. We must look to Him as our true north and our source of everlasting hope!

Scriptures to Think On:

Why are you cast down, O my soul? And why are you disquieted within me? Hope in God; For I shall yet praise Him… **Psalm 42:11a-b**

Now may the God of hope fill you with all joy and peace in believing, that you may abound in hope by the power of the Holy Spirit. **Romans 15:13**

JOURNAL

_____

_____

_____

_____

_____

_____

_____

_____

_____

_____

_____

_____

_____

_____

8. JOY

Joy can be difficult to define. We often get it confused with peace or happiness. We've all heard that joy is not synonymous with happiness, since the latter is based on our circumstances. But is that really true, especially in the midst of a crisis? Let us look at how that word "joy" is used in both the Hebrew and Greek.

The Hebrew word for "joy" in the Old Testament is often "simchah." It refers to singing, dancing, clapping of hands, and other similar expressions during festive occasions. These times of celebrations included seeing a loved one, hearing good news, release from prison, victory over an enemy, receiving great wealth, accomplishing a significant task, harvest, wedding, temple dedication, etc. The psalms are full of these expressions of rejoicing in God and promises of future rejoicing when God fulfills His covenant with His people.

The Greek word for "joy" in the New Testament is "chara." In the Gospels, it primarily refers to the celebration inaugurating the Messiah's coming. Other books in the New Testament expand its meaning to the experience of being "in Christ" and having the "fullness of the Spirit." Furthermore, the New Testament writers remind us that joy is not only meant for the good days but also for the tough days of suffering. The believer is to rejoice knowing that Christ is coming soon and find joy in spreading the gospel. Because of this, God's children don't need to wait to feel joy. We can choose to be joyful now!

So, what is joy? It's more than just a deep inner feeling. It's also an outward celebration of God's goodness. Sometimes, it's with others but it can also be expressed by ourselves. Joy transcends our circumstances because, as Christians, it is rooted in Jesus Christ and His gospel. When crises and troubles hit, we can lose many things. Most are material, but if we are born-again Christians, we cannot lose Jesus and we can still share the gospel.

And remember, having joy does not mean that we will never be sad or discouraged but the Holy Spirit will be there in the tough seasons to bear the fruit of joy in our lives. Even in times of discouragement, nothing can take away our joy. Take a moment today to rejoice in what God has done for you and how He has blessed you.

Scriptures to Think On:

You will show me the path of life; In Your presence is fullness of joy... **Psalm16:11a**

These things I have spoken to you, that My joy may remain in you, and that your joy may be full. **John 15:11**

My brethren, count it all joy when you fall into various trials. **James 1:2**

JOURNAL

_____

_____

_____

_____

_____

_____

_____

_____

_____

_____

_____

_____

_____

_____

9. FAITH

In times of crisis, it's hard to know who we can trust. Is the media telling the truth? Are politicians lying to us? Do the professionals really know what is happening or are they hiding things from us because they're unable to handle the crisis?

Unfortunately, we tend to transfer these doubts towards God. We begin to ask the age-old questions: Why is God not doing anything about this? Does He not know what's going on? Does He not care about what we're going through? Is He not powerful enough to handle this? In these times, we need a faith that will transcend our fears.

We need to remember that faith is not just wishful thinking or an optimistic outlook on life. It is the result of a deep personal relationship with God. Think about it: can we truly trust someone we don't know? Of course not! In the Old Testament, the word for "faith" or trust in Hebrew is "bethath," which means to lie helplessly face down. If we're going to have a faith that will outlast our crisis, it will require something far more than a half-hearted, wishy-washy looking to God. We will have to spend time with Him through His Word and prayer. Daily, maybe even hourly, we will have to lie helplessly facedown before Him. As we develop that kind of a relationship with Him, we will get to know His true nature and power. In the process, He will fill us with joy and peace, and we will overflow with hope by the power of the Holy Spirit. Paul assures us of this in

Romans 15:13 "Now may the God of hope fill you with all joy and peace in believing, that you may abound in hope by the power of the Holy Spirit."

What if we still struggle with our faith? Follow the example of the great inventor and entrepreneur, R. G. LeTourneau. Someone once asked him, "If you know a thing is the will of God, and you do not feel you have the faith, what do you do?" He answered, "I go ahead and act like I have the faith." When we have a deep personal relationship with God, we can say that too.

Scriptures to Think On:

You will keep him in perfect peace, whose mind is stayed on You, because he trusts in You. Trust in the LORD forever... **Isaiah 26:3-4a**

But without faith it is impossible to please Him, for he who comes to God must believe that He is, and that He is a rewarder of those who diligently seek Him. **Hebrews 11:6**

JOURNAL

_____

_____

_____

_____

_____

_____

_____

_____

_____

_____

_____

_____

_____

_____

10. STRENGTH

Our shoulders were never designed to bear the weight of a crisis. Small trials can be handled easily enough, but we're talking about major adversities that threaten to crush us. To quote Thomas Paine, "These are the times that try men's souls." No amount of "gritting our teeth" and "sucking it up" will get us through these times. Job recognized this in his crisis as he lamented, "What strength do I have, that I should hope?" (Job 6:11a) We need shoulders much stronger than ours to come alongside and carry the weight as we move forward.

Every crisis is an invitation for us to turn to God and rely on His strength rather than our own. He designed us to be dependent upon Him. To further clarify, we are not to ask God for strength but to invite God to be our strength. There is a big difference. This has always been the way God's people have seen their crises. Moses sang, "The LORD is my strength and song…" (Exodus 15:2a) The psalmist declared, "I will love You, O LORD, my strength" (Psalm 18:1), "God is our refuge and strength, a very present help in trouble" (Psalm 46:1), "My flesh and my heart fail; but God is the strength of my heart and my portion forever" (Psalm 73:26).

How do we see tough times in our lives? Some see them as opportunities to prove themselves. Others simply shrug their shoulders and concede. There are even those who become bitter and hopeless. We must choose to see our trials as opportunities for God to come alongside us and help carry the load. Choose to say with Paul, "Therefore I take pleasure in infirmities, in reproaches, in needs, in persecutions, in distresses, for Christ's sake. For when I am weak, then I am strong" (2 Corinthians 12:10).

Scriptures to Think On:

But those who wait on the LORD shall renew their strength; They shall mount up with wings like eagles, they shall run and not be weary, they shall walk and not faint. **Isaiah 40:31**

Finally, my brethren, be strong in the Lord and in the power of His might. **Ephesians 6:10**

JOURNAL

_____

_____

_____

_____

_____

_____

_____

_____

_____

_____

_____

_____

_____

11. RESOLVE

Some days, the crisis can be so overwhelming that we feel paralyzed, suffocating under the weight of hopelessness and despair. Daily tasks and important deadlines get ignored and apathy takes full control. No amount of Bible knowledge or motivational pep talks seem to help us get going. We ask ourselves, "What's the use of trying since it's not going to work?"

What do we do when we find ourselves infected with a case of "give-up-itis?" We learn from the examples of those who resolved to press on in spite of their circumstances. One example that comes to mind is that of Caleb, the 85-year old warrior. Caleb, when he was a younger man, was part of the group of spies who had gone into the Promised Land. Contrary to the others, he and his friend, Joshua, brought back a good report. Nevertheless, they were outvoted and had to wander 40 years in the wilderness with the others.

When it was finally time for the Israelites to re-enter the land, Caleb could have been negative or apathetic. He could have said, "I tried to tell you 40 years ago!" Instead, he told his old friend Joshua, "behold, the LORD has kept me alive…As yet I am as strong this day as on the day that Moses sent me; just as my strength was then, so now is my strength for war, both for going out and for coming in. Now therefore, give me this mountain of which the LORD spoke in that day" (Joshua 14:10-12).

31

But what about when we don't feel like being a "Caleb"? That's when we need to join the psalmist in saying "This is the day the Lord has made. We will rejoice and be glad in it" (Psalm 118:24). Do we truly believe that the Lord has made each day? When our life has been turned upside down as the result of a crisis, are we still willing to rejoice? In these days of uncertainty, let us resolve to look at each day as a gift from God. We have another day to serve God. We have another day to spend time with our family. We have another day to make an impact for God's Kingdom. Let us make the choice to rejoice in each day and to be glad. At the end of our lives, may we be able to look back on how we lived each day with no regrets.

Scriptures to Think On:

And let us not grow weary while doing good, for in due season we shall reap if we do not lose heart.   **Galatians 6:9**

Fight the good fight of faith, lay hold on eternal life…
1 Timothy 6:12a

Therefore, my beloved brethren, be steadfast, immovable, always abounding in the work of the Lord, knowing that your labor is not in vain in the Lord.
1 Corinthians 15:58

JOURNAL

12. SELF-CONTROL

Self-control is the one area in which even the best of us fail, especially during a crisis. It usually manifests itself in two different ways.

First, when our emotions are going haywire, we say and do things to those near us that we wouldn't do normally. This behavior causes grief and damage that takes ages to heal and sometimes never does.

Second, our lack of self-control can manifest itself in self-destructive behavior. Due to self-pity and hopelessness, people turn to self-indulgences like overeating, binge watching, and reckless spending. This results in devastating effects to our health, mind, and finances. Both the outward and inward manifestations of indiscipline can be irreparable, if left unchecked.

The key to fostering self-control is to recognize that the source of our problem is internal. We want to blame our circumstances, other people, or the fact that we live in a broken world for our struggles when the root cause is us. Just as we teach our children that there are consequences for their actions, God does the same with His people. He wants us to be obedient and exercise self-control so that we can reap the blessings of a holy life.

Thankfully, God has not left us helpless but has given us the Holy Spirit to guide us when we are tempted to lose self-control. He reminds us that we are not in charge of our lives but Christ is and we are to obey Him. For us to lose control in our lives is to usurp God's rule. Self-control is really about remembering Christ-control. Next time you are tempted to lash out or self-destruct, ask yourself, "Who is truly in control of my mind and my heart right now?" It will help you control what you think, say, and do.

Scriptures to Think On:

Whoever has no rule over his own spirit is like a city broken down, without walls. **Proverbs 25:28**

For the good that I will to do, I do not do; but the evil I will not to do, that I practice....O wretched man that I am! Who will deliver me from this body of death? I thank God—through Jesus Christ our Lord! **Romans 7:19, 24-25**

But the fruit of the Spirit is love, joy, peace, longsuffering, kindness, goodness, faithfulness, gentleness, self-control. **Galatians 5:22-23**

JOURNAL

_____

_____

_____

_____

_____

_____

_____

_____

_____

_____

_____

_____

_____

_____

13. COURAGE

One of my all-time favorite movies is the Wizard of Oz. As a child, I (Nicole) always loved the Cowardly Lion. Even though he acts bravely in the face of fear, he still thinks that he lacks courage. The Lion has to be reminded by the Wizard at the end that he is, in fact, courageous. So also, during a crisis, we need to be reminded that our courage is not the absence of fear. Instead, it is stepping out in spite of fear. For some of us, this feels like a foreign concept, especially if our current crisis has left us fearful and anxious.

How, then, can we live courageously in spite of fear? For starters, it helps to be around courageous people. We become like the people closest to us. Moses was a courageous leader, and as he passed the baton of leadership on to Joshua, Moses reminded him, "Have I not commanded you? Be strong and of good courage; do not be afraid, nor be dismayed, for the LORD your God is with you wherever you go" (Joshua 1:9). Joshua demonstrated incredible courage as he led the people of Israel to conquer the Promised Land. His mentor's words had a profound impact on the way he conducted himself in the face of danger.

Next, we need to be reminded of what is at stake if we fail to conquer our fear. Paul instructed the Philippians, "Only let your conduct be worthy of the gospel of Christ...and not in any way terrified by your adversaries, which is to them a proof of perdition, but to you of salvation, and that from God" (Philippians 1:27-28). In other words, courage is the mark of a gospel-centered life.

There may be times when there's no one around to breathe courage into you. What then? In those moments, learn from David, who in the face of being stoned by his own people, "strengthened himself in the Lord his God" (1 Samuel 30:6d).

Living in enemy territory takes courage. Reaching out and rescuing people from eternal destruction takes courage. Stepping out in faith to what God is calling us to do takes courage. This courage is not in ourselves and our abilities, but in the power of the Holy Spirit who lives in us. In order to develop courage, God will lead us through situations that give us the opportunity to rely on His strength.

Scriptures to Think On:

And David said to his son Solomon, 'Be strong and of good courage, and do it; do not fear nor be dismayed, for the LORD God—my God—will be with you. He will not leave you nor forsake you...' **1 Chronicles 28:20**

And He was withdrawn from them about a stone's throw, and He knelt down and prayed, saying, 'Father, if it is Your will, take this cup away from Me; nevertheless, not My will, but Yours, be done.' Then an angel appeared to Him from heaven, strengthening Him. **Luke 22:41-43**

For God has not given us a spirit of fear, but of power and of love and of a sound mind. **2 Timothy 1:7**

JOURNAL

_____

_____

_____

_____

_____

_____

_____

_____

_____

_____

_____

_____

_____

_____

14. PATIENCE

No one going through a crisis ever thinks, "This is a perfect time for this to happen." Crises, by nature, are inconvenient and disruptive. Our daily routine gets upended, our natural abilities become limited, and all of our valuable resources get depleted or temporarily put on hold. We sit around and wait for something to change or, even worse, wait on other people to change it for us. Most of us don't handle waiting very well. Instead, we wallow in self-pity, we complain, and even lash out in anger and frustration. We need patience.

But patience is much more than the ability to "just hang in there." It's also the attitude we display while we hang in there. Think about it: What's so great about "hanging in there" if we try to hang everybody else in the process? Instead, we are to demonstrate an attitude that will allow God to do His deep work in our lives during our crisis. As James reminds us, "let patience have its perfect work, that you may be perfect and complete, lacking nothing" (James 1:4). This may also allow God to do a deep work in the lives of those around us.

Ultimately, we should view our crisis through the eyes of eternity. As Paul told the Corinthians, "For our light affliction, which is but for a moment, is working for us a far more exceeding and eternal weight of glory" (2 Corinthians 4:17). In other words, having to be patient is not a punishment, but a preparation for God's greater purpose.

Patience, ultimately, is an opportunity for God to prepare us for eternity.

Scriptures to Think On:

Rest in the LORD, and wait patiently for Him; Do not fret because of him who prospers in his way, because of the man who brings wicked schemes to pass.   **Proverbs 37:7**

Be kindly affectionate to one another with brotherly love, in honor giving preference to one another; not lagging in diligence, fervent in spirit, serving the Lord; rejoicing in hope, patient in tribulation, continuing steadfastly in prayer. **Romans 12:10-12**

JOURNAL

_____

_____

_____

_____

_____

_____

_____

_____

_____

_____

_____

_____

_____

_____

15. DIRECTION

How did we ever survive before GPS? It was somewhere in the mid-2000s that Abidan and I first heard about this technology and it has revolutionized our lives ever since! Prior to that, I can't tell you how many evenings we spent parked on the side of the road, tracing lines on an old, torn-up atlas, trying to find our destination. Now, all we have to do is type in the address and the phone does the rest.

If only we had a GPS to get us through the crises of life. How wonderful would it be if a voice could just tell us where to turn and when to stop. We could sit back and steer our way out of the storm. During a crisis, we are bombarded with a myriad of voices that seem to be providing direction, but in reality, they often lead to pain and heartache. This can be overwhelming and extremely hazardous. How can we make sure that we are listening to the right directions? How do we successfully navigate a crisis?

To start with, we need to take the time to get alone with God. It is imperative that we hear His voice first and for as long as possible. The more we become acclimated to God's tone and tenor, the faster we will recognize who around us is speaking for God and who is simply speaking. Next, we need to spend time in His Word. The best way to recognize a counterfeit is by studying the legitimate. Finally, we need to take the time to develop a relationship with godly, mature adults that we can turn to when times are hard. Just as Ruth had Naomi and Timothy had Paul, we all need gender-specific godly mentors who can serve as God's GPS for our lives.

Do you feel lost in your crisis? Do you feel panic rising in your chest? Do you feel that the world is closing in around you? Reread this paragraph and notice the word that is repeated: "feel." Feelings are not always reliable. Never make decisions based on your emotions. Choose to follow the truth. As someone has said, "Feelings are the shallowest part of our being." This concept is especially hard for women. I'm sure ladies would agree with me that most of us are emotional creatures. Unfortunately, our feelings can be misleading. Instead, we should make every effort to follow Jesus. He is the Way, the Truth, and the Life. He will never mislead us, especially in a crisis.

Scriptures to Think On:

Then Moses called Joshua and said to him in the sight of all Israel, 'Be strong and of good courage, for you must go with this people to the land which the LORD has sworn to their fathers to give them, and you shall cause them to inherit it. And the LORD, He is the One who goes before you. He will be with you, He will not leave you nor forsake you; do not fear nor be dismayed.' **Deuteronomy 31:7-8**

Imitate me, just as I also imitate Christ. **1 Corinthians 11:1**

JOURNAL

_____

_____

_____

_____

_____

_____

_____

_____

_____

_____

_____

_____

_____

_____

16. AUTHORITIES

Certain crises may cause us to be placed under special constraints by the authorities. Having our everyday life interrupted or restricted is unnerving. We may even feel threatened and vulnerable, as though our fundamental rights and freedoms are under attack. How should we respond in such situations?

Of course, we should begin with prayer. Paul urges us in 1 Timothy 2:1-2, "I exhort first of all that supplications, prayers, intercessions, and giving of thanks be made for...all who are in authority, that we may lead a quiet and peaceable life in all godliness and reverence." Prayer has a way of softening our attitude towards those in authority, even when we disagree with their decisions. Next, we should remember that every authority in our lives has been appointed by God—"Let every soul be subject to the governing authorities. For there is no authority except from God, and the authorities that exist are appointed by God" (Romans 13:1).

Finally, we should remember that our response towards those in authority can validate or invalidate the gospel— "For this is the will of God, that by doing good you may put to silence the ignorance of foolish men—as free, yet not using liberty as a cloak for vice, but as bondservants of God" (1 Peter 2:15-16).

Sometimes, there may be concerns that our fundamental rights and freedoms are being increasingly restricted without valid reasons. History shows us time and again that the lost world, especially those in authority, is never neutral or fair towards God's people. That's why, as believers, it is our responsibility to vote for representatives that will be most supportive of our values. This is not because the government can solve all our problems or bring about God's kingdom on earth, but because the right government can protect our rights as Christians to live out our convictions and share our faith. However, if there is tangible proof that the authorities have ulterior motives for their decisions instead of our best intentions, then we have the right and the obligation to resist and vote them out of office.

Scriptures to Think On:

Obey those who rule over you, and be submissive, for they watch out for your souls, as those who must give account. Let them do so with joy and not with grief, for that would be unprofitable for you. **Hebrews 13:17**

For rulers are not a terror to good works, but to evil. Do you want to be unafraid of the authority? Do what is good, and you will have praise from the same. For he is God's minister to you for good. But if you do evil, be afraid; for he does not bear the sword in vain; for he is God's minister, an avenger to execute wrath on him who practices evil. Therefore you must be subject, not only because of wrath but also for conscience' sake. For because of this you also pay taxes, for they are God's ministers attending continually to this very thing. Render therefore to all their due: taxes to whom taxes are due, customs to whom customs, fear to whom fear, honor to whom honor. **Romans 13:3-7**

JOURNAL

_____

_____

_____

_____

_____

_____

_____

_____

_____

_____

_____

_____

_____

17. COMMUNITY

We were made for community. After God made Adam and put him in the Garden of Eden, He saw the man's loneliness and declared, "It is not good that man should be alone..." We need others to walk with us, especially when times are tough. Self-isolation may be okay for a short while, but failure to connect with others leads to distractedness, despair, and even depression. Christians are not immune to this. Yes, we can pray and grow in the Word, but community is not optional.

The early church modeled community for all of us. Acts 2:46-47 says, "They worshiped together at the Temple each day, met in homes for the Lord's Supper, and shared their meals with great joy and generosity—all the while praising God and enjoying the goodwill of the people. And each day the Lord added to their fellowship those who were being saved." During a crisis, churches may not always be able to meet in their usual way (in a building) but be certain of one thing: we are still the body of Christ.

In this day and age, technology allows us to keep in contact with each other. We should take advantage of these mediums and reach out to our local body of Christ. Touching base with each other will get our minds off of ourselves and onto others. We need to let people know we are praying for them.

Having said that, technology is no substitute for face-to-face connection. Neglecting to gather in person in a physical location should never become the new norm. Some people seem to relish the isolation, but this is not biblical Christianity. Every effort should be made to come together again as soon as possible. The strength of the church lies in our ability to stand physically together in the face of crises.

Scriptures to Think On:

But if we walk in the light as He is in the light, we have fellowship with one another, and the blood of Jesus Christ His Son cleanses us from all sin.   **1 John 1:7**

Bear one another's burdens, and so fulfill the law of Christ.   **Galatians 6:1-2**

And let us consider one another in order to stir up love and good works, not forsaking the assembling of ourselves together, as is the manner of some, but exhorting one another, and so much the more as you see the Day approaching.   **Hebrews 10:24-25**

JOURNAL

_____

_____

_____

_____

_____

_____

_____

_____

_____

_____

_____

_____

_____

18. FOCUS

During times of crises, we tend to lose our focus or worse, we focus on the wrong things. Unfortunately, in our hyper-connected world, that's becoming easier and easier. All it takes is one shocking news headline or one jarring Facebook or Instagram post, and before we know it, we've wasted hours researching a topic that accomplished nothing.

In a sports game, when the players begin to lose their momentum, the coach calls a timeout to talk to them. So also, in the game of life, the Holy Spirit calls a timeout to talk to us, to remind us about the game plan. He warns us about how much time we have left. He corrects our mistakes. And above all, He gives us the right focus to get back in the game and win it!

As you go about your day today, think about the list that Paul gave the Philippians in his letter: "whatever things are true, whatever things are noble, whatever things are just, whatever things are pure, whatever things are lovely, whatever things are of good report, if there is any virtue and if there is anything praiseworthy—meditate on these things" (Philippians 4:8).

If you realize that your focus is on something negative, go back to this verse and train your mind to focus on Paul's list. All those what-if's that swirl within our own mind can also hold us captive if we aren't careful to take hold of every thought and turn them over to God first. As we shift our focus from the lies that Satan throws at us to the truth of God's Word, our perception of the world will change. We will begin to see God working all around us, and He is worthy of our focus and our praise! Let us allow Him to refocus our attention back on His Word.

Scriptures to Think On:

Let your eyes look straight ahead, and your eyelids look right before you. Ponder the path of your feet, and let all your ways be established. Do not turn to the right or the left; remove your foot from evil.   **Proverbs 4:25-27**

Not that I have already attained, or am already perfected; but I press on, that I may lay hold of that for which Christ Jesus has also laid hold of me. Brethren, I do not count myself to have apprehended; but one thing I do, forgetting those things which are behind and reaching forward to those things which are ahead, I press toward the goal for the prize of the upward call of God in Christ Jesus. **Philippians 3:12-14**

JOURNAL

_____

_____

_____

_____

_____

_____

_____

_____

_____

_____

_____

_____

_____

_____

19. SERVICE

It's no accident that in times of crises, we see the worst of human nature. Instead of demonstrating compassion toward others, people grab, snatch, and claw their way to whatever they want without any regard for others--even for something as trivial as toilet paper! Why do people behave like this? Could it be that, under pressure, our true nature reveals itself?

As believers, we are called to demonstrate Christ during times of crisis. While the world is resorting to selfishness, we are to serve others in the name of Jesus. This has always been the mark of believers. When people would abandon their families and neighbors because of a plague or epidemic, Christians stayed behind to care for those who couldn't care for themselves. Even today, Christian missionaries and relief workers go places where others would never set foot. Why? Because we are called to be the Good Samaritan who took care of the Jewish man, his sworn enemy. There is no greater antidote for selfishness than acts of service toward others.

Let us take a look at our own lives. How are we serving others during times of crisis? Chances are, there are people around us who are going through something worse than we can possibly imagine. Are we willing to step out of our comfort zone and be the light of Christ in a dark world for someone? Serving others will not only put our own suffering in perspective, but it will also serve as an antidote to pride and selfishness. Today, we must stop asking God why we are going through our crises and begin asking Him to show us opportunities to serve others.

Scriptures to Think On:

But love your enemies, do good, and lend, hoping for nothing in return; and your reward will be great, and you will be sons of the Most High. For He is kind to the unthankful and evil. Therefore be merciful, just as your Father also is merciful. **Luke 6:35-36**

But whoever desires to become great among you shall be your servant. And whoever of you desires to be first shall be slave of all. For even the Son of Man did not come to be served, but to serve, and to give His life a ransom for many. **Mark 10:43b-45**

Pure and undefiled religion before God and the Father is this: to visit orphans and widows in their trouble, and to keep oneself unspotted from the world. **James 1:27**

JOURNAL

_____

_____

_____

_____

_____

_____

_____

_____

_____

_____

_____

_____

_____

_____

20. RESPONSIBILITY

Most of us consider ourselves responsible. We execute our daily tasks with determination, taking comfort in knowing what is expected of us. However, nothing disrupts our routine like a crisis. It preoccupies our mind from the moment our feet hit the floor, until we get back in bed. All day, we become obsessed with searching and scrolling, finding out a little more about what's going on in the world. This was the case after September 11, 2001. Day after day, millions of Americans stayed glued to the TV. Today, it's even worse. We get minute-by-minute updates through notifications from the news and one more quick scroll on social media. Unfortunately, this negatively impacts our daily chores, work, health, relationships, and spiritual life.

How do we guard against these consequences? For starters, we need to trust God's sovereignty over the crisis. Checking the news constantly may feel satisfying at the moment, but it doesn't change the outcome. Jesus reminded us in Luke 12:25-26, "Which of you by worrying can add one cubit to his stature? If you then are not able to do the least, why are you anxious for the rest?" We must trust that God is well aware of what's going on in our lives and is perfectly in control when the TV is off or the phone is left alone. Unplug from your information sources and ask God to remind you of His sovereignty.

Next, we need to take responsibility for the tasks that need to be accomplished. Although there is a storm going on around us, we still have things that must get done. From work to caring for our families, we must persevere, even though it would be easier to blame others or wallow in self-pity. Make a list, set reminders, and begin each task with determination and a sense of responsibility. Time that we lose cannot be returned to us. Paul warns us: "See then that you walk circumspectly, not as fools but as wise, redeeming the time, because the days are evil" (Ephesians 5:15-16). God has given us each day to do His work. Let us redeem that time for His glory.

Scriptures to Think On:

So teach us to number our days, that we may gain a heart of wisdom. **Psalm 90:12**

I must work the works of Him who sent Me while it is day; the night is coming when no one can work. **John 9:4**

JOURNAL

_____

_____

_____

_____

_____

_____

_____

_____

_____

_____

_____

_____

_____

_____

21. BURDEN BEARING

What does it mean to bear a burden? It sounds like something most of us would rather avoid. We are not talking about that kind of a burden bearing. Neither are we talking about coming alongside someone and helping with their struggles. Although that is important—we are commanded to do so in Scriptures—what we are referring to here is bearing with those who may not agree with your take on the crisis.

Sometimes, people are adamant that their view is the only valid position and anyone who doesn't agree wholeheartedly is an enemy. There's nothing wrong with others making a case for their views, but we are also free to stand firm on our own convictions and refuse to compromise. Nonetheless, bearing with others allows us to disagree without becoming disagreeable. In other words, we are not talking about our conviction but the way we conduct ourselves when we disagree. This happens a lot within families. One side disagrees with the other and becomes mean and hateful in the process. It never helps and it sours our testimony to believers and unbelievers.

Bearing a burden requires wisdom. It is actually wiser to take the time to see the other person's perspective than it is to stubbornly insist that you're right. Not only does it change the tone of the conversation, but it also creates opportunities to present our case more effectively. Who knows? We may actually see the merit of the other side in the process. Regardless, even if the disagreement persists, it will certainly make us more winsome in the eyes of the other person and keep the door open for future conversations.

Jesus demonstrated this in the Gospel of John. Remember His interaction with Mary and Martha. Even though they failed to recognize His authority over death, He did not condemn them. Instead, He met them where they were spiritually. To the contrary, the scribes and the Pharisees were adamantly unwilling to bear with others. Just like Jesus, we should be willing to meet people where they are instead of condemning them. In the process, we will learn what it means to "bear with one another." Let that impact the way we interact with others today.

Scriptures to Think On:

I, therefore, the prisoner of the Lord, beseech you to walk worthy of the calling with which you were called, with all lowliness and gentleness, with longsuffering, bearing with one another in love. **Ephesians 4:1-2**

Therefore, as the elect of God, holy and beloved, put on tender mercies, kindness, humility, meekness, longsuffering; bearing with one another, and forgiving one another, if anyone has a complaint against another; even as Christ forgave you, so you also must do. **Colossians 3:12-13**

JOURNAL

22. CHANGE

Most of us are creatures of habit, meaning that we love our routine. If change is required of us, we ease into it, slowly making room for it in our lives. Unfortunately, in times of crisis, change is the first guest to show up at our doorstep, ready to move into our lives whether we like it or not. It has no regard for our daily routine or our comfort, and it starts making immediate and unreasonable demands. Now, every day becomes a fight against this unwelcome and obnoxious visitor. And, guess what? It has no intention of leaving.

In times like these, we have to learn to adjust to a new normal. This is a difficult process, but a necessary one if we are to weather the crisis. It begins by taking stock of what really matters: the non-negotiables. Reading the Bible and praying every day should be at the top of that list. No matter what changes in our lives, our daily time with God must remain constant in order to help us navigate the new normal. Although there may be days when this time doesn't seem convenient or essential, to compromise here is to fail everywhere else. Our time with God puts other things in life, especially the unwelcome changes, into proper perspective. He will help us with the wisdom, strength, grace, courage, love, and self-control we need to handle the change.

But this change can also be a blessing in disguise. Sometimes, we get locked into habits which are not healthy or helpful for anyone. Could this be the time in which God is shaking us out of our comfort zones so we can find His true purpose for us? Today, we must ask God to not only help us navigate this time of change, but to use it as a way to align us with His will for our lives and the world.

Scriptures to Think On:

To everything there is a season, a time for every purpose under heaven: A time to be born, and a time to die; a time to plant, and a time to pluck what is planted; a time to kill, and a time to heal; a time to break down, and a time to build up; a time to weep, and a time to laugh; a time to mourn, and a time to dance; a time to cast away stones, and a time to gather stones; a time to embrace, and a time to refrain from embracing; a time to gain, and a time to lose; a time to keep, and a time to throw away; a time to tear, and a time to sew; a time to keep silence, and a time to speak; a time to love, and a time to hate; a time of war, and a time of peace. **Ecclesiastes 3:1-8**

Jesus Christ is the same yesterday, today, and forever. **Hebrews 13:8**

JOURNAL

_____

_____

_____

_____

_____

_____

_____

_____

_____

_____

_____

_____

_____

23. PROTECTION

No one likes to be vulnerable. We all prefer to feel like everything is under control, with no visible signs of weakness. But there's no denying that crises make us vulnerable. When our world is turned upside down, our foundations are loosened, our securities come unhinged, and fear begins to rule our lives. We wake up every day, heavy in the stomach, not knowing what we may have to face. We dread the silence of night and feel like we'll never see the sunrise on a new day again.

In times like these, we need solid assurance that we will make it to the other side. We need to be reminded that nothing can reach us without first coming through the hands of God. Jesus said in John 10:27-29, "My sheep hear My voice, and I know them, and they follow Me. And I give them eternal life, and they shall never perish; neither shall anyone snatch them out of My hand. My Father, who has given them to Me, is greater than all; and no one is able to snatch them out of My Father's hand." In other words, for anything to happen to us, it must be allowed by both the Father and the Son.

During crises, the real battle is in our minds. It is only through surrendering our anxious thoughts to God and allowing Him to fight on our behalf that we can find victory. Hence, it is imperative that we bring "every thought into captivity to the obedience of Christ" (2 Corinthians 10:5). As Christ rules our thoughts, worry and anxiety have no place to enter into our minds.

Scriptures to Think On:

Behold, He who keeps Israel shall neither slumber nor sleep. The LORD is your keeper; The LORD is your shade at your right hand. The sun shall not strike you by day, nor the moon by night. The LORD shall preserve you from all evil; He shall preserve your soul. The LORD shall preserve your going out and your coming in from this time forth, and even forevermore. **Psalm 121:1**

No weapon formed against you shall prosper, and every tongue which rises against you in judgment you shall condemn. This is the heritage of the servants of the LORD... **Isaiah 54:17**

My sheep hear My voice, and I know them, and they follow Me. And I give them eternal life, and they shall never perish; neither shall anyone snatch them out of My hand... **John 10:27-29**

But the Lord is faithful, who will establish you and guard you from the evil one. **2 Thessalonians 3:3**

JOURNAL

24. FINANCES

Most people don't know how to live within their means. This becomes painfully obvious during times of crisis. Unplanned expenses barge in like hospital visits, unexpected childcare, extra trips to the grocery stores, unemployment, disabilities, etc. Such financial problems can become a major source of conflict in our relationships, especially marriage. If not handled properly and timely, they can cause permanent damage.

To begin with, financial security requires wisdom, hard work, discipline, and foresight. Thankfully, the Bible has the answer to all of these issues, specifically the Book of Proverbs, "Go to the ant, you sluggard! Consider her ways and be wise, which, having no captain, overseer or ruler, provides her supplies in the summer, and gathers her food in the harvest. How long will you slumber, O sluggard? When will you rise from your sleep? A little sleep, a little slumber, a little folding of the hands to sleep—So shall your poverty come on you like a prowler, and your need like an armed man" (Proverbs 6:6-11).

In chemistry, a litmus test is often used to determine the acidity of a substance. When it comes into contact with the material being tested, the litmus strip changes color based on the pH level of that substance. Money is the litmus test of our faith, showing us our level of trust in God regarding our finances. We prove our trust in God by giving our gifts and offerings to Him, especially during times of crisis. This will be challenging, but by giving it away, we are declaring that the One who controls our lives is God alone. As we know, God doesn't need our money. He is only looking for our act of obedience and trust. In the process, He will bless us many times over. I (Abidan) can remember my parents teaching me that concept from an early age, and it has proven to be true time and again.

Finally, crisis is also an eye-opener to show us what really matters to us. As Jesus said, "For where your treasure is, there your heart will be also" (Matthew 6:21). Is your heart on earthly things that will not last or on heavenly things that will last forever? Use crises as opportunities to examine your heart's treasure and reinvest accordingly.

Scriptures to Think On:

Will a man rob God? Yet you have robbed Me! But you say, 'In what way have we robbed You?' In tithes and offerings. You are cursed with a curse, for you have robbed Me, even this whole nation. Bring all the tithes into the storehouse, that there may be food in My house, and try Me now in this," says the Lord of hosts, "If I will not open for you the windows of heaven and pour out for you such blessing that there will not be room enough to receive it. And I will rebuke the devourer for your sakes, so that he will not destroy the fruit of your ground, nor shall the vine fail to bear fruit for you in the field," says the Lord of hosts.
Malachi 3:8-11

Command those who are rich in this present age not to be haughty, nor to trust in uncertain riches but in the living God, who gives us richly all things to enjoy. Let them do good, that they be rich in good works, ready to give, willing to share, storing up for themselves a good foundation for the time to come, that they may lay hold on eternal life.
1 Timothy 6:17-19

JOURNAL

_____

_____

_____

_____

_____

_____

_____

_____

_____

_____

_____

_____

_____

25. UNDERSTANDING

We've all felt at times that no one understands what we are going through. This becomes even more pronounced when we are in the midst of a crisis. Although our struggles are unique and painful to us, it's untrue that no one understands. There is One who always understands: His name is Jesus. There is no situation known to any human being to which He cannot relate. He was fully God who became fully man so He could die in our place, but there's more. The reason He lived 33 years before He went to the cross was so that He could truly relate to us and help us in our time of need. Here are just a few things we deal with that Jesus understands:

If we're hungry? Jesus spent forty days and nights fasting in the wilderness.
If we're thirsty? From the cross Jesus cried, "I thirst."
If we're exhausted? Jesus and His disciples did not even have time to eat or sleep because of the multitude.
If we're struggling with temptation? Jesus was harassed by the Devil himself.
If we're homeless? Jesus said in Luke 9:58 "…Foxes have holes and birds of the air have nests, but the Son of Man has nowhere to lay His head."
If we're mocked? Jesus was ridiculed for His family background and place of origin.
If we're grieved? Jesus had compassion on the grieving

widow who had lost her only son and He brought him back to life.

If we're angry? Jesus got angry at the Pharisees who tried to use the sickness of a man to trap Him into healing on the Sabbath.

If we're having family trouble? Jesus' brothers refused to believe in Him.

If we're afraid for our life? Jesus had to avoid Judea because His enemies were trying to kill Him.

If we're lonely and feel betrayed? One of His own disciples betrayed Him and the rest forsook Him and fled.

If we're falsely accused? Jesus was falsely accused on the night before He was crucified.

If we're in physical pain? Jesus was scourged and a crown of thorns was thrust upon His head. Then, He was crucified between two thieves.

Someone might say that Jesus does not understand what marital trouble is like since He never married. True, Jesus did not have an earthly wife, but He was in a covenant relationship with His people Israel in the Old Testament. He knows what it means to have someone cheat on Him. Furthermore, the church is now called the Bride of Christ. But, how about wayward children? He gets it. After all, He gave the parable of the Prodigal Son.

The point is that He understands whatever we go through and He is willing to meet our needs.

Scripture to Think On:

Therefore, in all things He had to be made like His brethren, that He might be a merciful and faithful High Priest... **Hebrews 2:17**

JOURNAL

_____

_____

_____

_____

_____

_____

_____

_____

_____

_____

_____

_____

_____

26. LAUGHTER

Crisis has a way of turning our smiles into sighs, our gladness into gloom, and our laughter into lament. In times such as these, laughter is exactly what the doctor has ordered. Experts have shown through various studies over the years that laughter has many benefits: it releases endorphins, lowers the blood pressure, improves the immune system, decreases stress, and it can even give us a fresh perspective on our problem! Is it any wonder that God has given us the gift of laughter?

We often portray Jesus as a mopey, forlorn figure because Scripture refers to him as "a man of sorrows and acquainted with grief" (Isaiah 53:3b). But this is not an accurate portrait. Yes, His heart was broken over the depravity of human beings, but His heart was also full of joy. Think about who constantly surrounded Him. Fishermen, tax collectors, prostitutes, and the vast multitude of common people. These groups were known for their lightheartedness! He used many Hebrew expressions like "whitewashed tombs" and "camel through the eye of a needle," as sarcasm in order to make His point about the overly-serious religious leaders. Let us not forget that Jesus was often surrounded by children. Do you think kids would flock to someone who was sad and morose? Of course not!

In his classic work, The Humor of Christ, Elton Trueblood remarked, "Far from laughter being incompatible with anguish, it is often the natural expression of deep pain." Let us take the time to see the humor in situations and let laughter open the pressure relief valve we all desperately need. Not only will laughter help you through a crisis, but it will lighten the load of those around you as well. But, be aware that when we try to laugh during a crisis, we may get chastised by those who feel as though stress and grief should remain throughout the day. In those times, laugh anyways!

Scriptures to Think On:

To everything there is a season, a time for every purpose under heaven...A time to weep, and a time to laugh; a time to mourn, and a time to dance. **Ecclesiastes 3:1-4**

Blessed are you who weep now, for you shall laugh. **Luke 6:21b**

JOURNAL

_____

_____

_____

_____

_____

_____

_____

_____

_____

_____

_____

_____

_____

_____

27. REST

Have you noticed yourself feeling more tired during days of uncertainty? Crises have a strange way of making us feel fatigued. In many cases, the mental strain that follows a sudden change in lifestyle is far worse than the physical. For example, worrying about bills or loss of a job can make us feel exhausted. We can also add the constant bombardment from news and social media! No wonder we're so mentally and emotionally drained. And the craziest thing? Those are the very mediums that we turn to in order to relax!

We need rest. Getting away to a relaxing beach or a beautiful log cabin in the mountains can do wonders for us. Unfortunately, in some crises, that's not always an option. We have to stay where we are, continue with what we are doing, and still somehow find ways to rest. What does that look like?

To start with, we must disconnect from technology and entertainment, even for short periods of time. Take the time to connect with the loved ones near you. Find that book you've been meaning to read, settle into a quiet room, and get lost in its words. Those among us who are not readers may want to work in the yard or the garage, but keep it light. The goal is to unwind.

And don't forget the more essential spiritual rest which only Christ can provide, as He said – "Come to Me, all you who labor and are heavy laden, and I will give you rest" (Matthew 11:28). Let us give every burden to God. He is more than capable of carrying them. His shoulders are far stronger and wider than ours. Then, let us take His yoke, which is easy and light.

Scriptures to Think On:

And He said, "My Presence will go with you, and I will give you rest." **Exodus 33:14**

For I have satiated the weary soul, and I have replenished every sorrowful soul. **Jeremiah 31:25**

Come to Me, all you who labor and are heavy laden, and I will give you rest. Take My yoke upon you and learn from Me, for I am gentle and lowly in heart, and you will find rest for your souls. For My yoke is easy and My burden is light. **Matthew 11:28-30**

And He said to them, "Come aside by yourselves to a deserted place and rest a while." For there were many coming and going, and they did not even have time to eat. **Mark 6:31**

JOURNAL

_____

_____

_____

_____

_____

_____

_____

_____

_____

_____

_____

_____

_____

28. HEALTH

When we become stressed, anxious, or otherwise preoccupied, often one of the first things to get neglected is our physical health. Crises interrupt our daily routine and we become more focused on navigating through uncertainty than taking good care of ourselves. Exercise, good nutrition, and a full night's sleep are on the way out, and emotional eating, junk food, and insomnia are here to stay!

A lot of the health issues we deal with are indicative of crisis and trauma in our lives. It's a vicious cycle where our health issues impact our mind and vice versa. Eventually, the two become inseparable, and it becomes difficult to determine whether the root issues lie in our physical or mental well-being.

We need to begin by correcting the common misconception that the body is not as important as the mind. God has designed us as a combination of immaterial (mind) and material (body), wherein the mind is not superior to the body or the body just a shell to house the mind. Every one of us is a mind-and-body unit; both are critical to make us who we are.

For believers, this takes on a special significance—"Or do you not know that your body is the temple of the Holy Spirit who is in you, whom you have from God, and you are not your own?" (1 Corinthians 6:19).

God deems our bodies extremely important and even promises a future transformation—"For our citizenship is in heaven, from which we also eagerly wait for the Savior, the Lord Jesus Christ, who will transform our lowly body that it may be conformed to His glorious body..." (Philippians 3:20-21a).

We also need to keep in mind that exercise and healthy foods help to reduce stress. In times of crisis, when stress begins to mount, we should take a walk or do our favorite workout. This will reduce stress, and, in turn, we will have more confidence and have a more positive perspective on our crisis. Simultaneously, let us not neglect our spiritual diet and exercise. When we fill our minds with junk, it's easy to feel sluggish, hopeless, or even depressed. But when our minds are full of the truth of God, we tend to feel better about ourselves, others, and our circumstances. We also tend to make wiser decisions in every area of our lives.

Scriptures to Think On:

Beloved, I pray that you may prosper in all things and be in health, just as your soul prospers. **3 John 2**

For bodily exercise profits a little, but godliness is profitable for all things. **1 Timothy 4:8**

JOURNAL

_____

_____

_____

_____

_____

_____

_____

_____

_____

_____

_____

_____

_____

_____

29. OPPORTUNITY

We've all heard that old adage: "Necessity is the mother of invention." This is especially true during times of crises when our daily activities are restricted, but we know we must continue to persevere in our work, caring for our family, etc. While some may simply adjust to the restrictions and relinquish their daily comforts, others harness them as an opportunity to improvise and even invent. In some ways, we can also say, "Crisis is the twin-sister of invention."

Think about the format in which early Christians read the Bible. They used scrolls, which were handed down through generations as part of their Jewish heritage. Can you imagine how difficult it must have been cross-referencing those texts, especially during preaching? Try unrolling from Isaiah all the way to Acts! So also, transportation would have been a nightmare, especially for Christians who were constantly on the run from persecution.

Then, someone came up with the idea of a "codex," or a book. Now, one could go from one book of the Scriptures to the next with just a turn of the page, rather than carrying around heavy, bulky, tangled up scrolls. Scholars still debate as to whether or not Christians invented the codex, but nonetheless, early manuscript evidence shows that they began using it from the earliest times. The ability to invent and create comes from being made in the image of God, the Great Creator. As image-bearers, we have the capacity to arrive at creative solutions to make life better for us and for others.

Crises can also be opportunities to spread the gospel in fresh, creative, and more effective ways. But be aware that there will be those who may oppose and try to discourage us. Let God fuel our passion and imagination in order to infuse our crises with creativity and ingenuity. This will not only help those around us, but will make us more like Him!

Scriptures to Think On:

And Moses said to the children of Israel, "See, the LORD has called by name Bezalel the son of Uri, the son of Hur, of the tribe of Judah; and He has filled him with the Spirit of God, in wisdom and understanding, in knowledge and all manner of workmanship, to design artistic works, to work in gold and silver and bronze, in cutting jewels for setting, in carving wood, and to work in all manner of artistic workmanship. And He has put in his heart the ability to teach, in him and Aholiab the son of Ahisamach, of the tribe of Dan. He has filled them with skill to do all manner of work of the engraver and the designer and the tapestry maker, in blue, purple, and scarlet thread, and fine linen, and of the weaver—those who do every work and those who design artistic works." **Exodus 35:30-35**

All things were made through Him, and without Him nothing was made that was made. **John 1:3**

JOURNAL

_____

_____

_____

_____

_____

_____

_____

_____

_____

_____

_____

_____

_____

_____

30. RESTART

Throughout this devotional, we've looked at words that play a major role in our lives during crises. In order to emerge victorious, it would be ideal if we could hit perfect 10's on each of them, but that's not possible in this fallen world. There will be days when we will feel really good about how we are doing and then there will be days that we will feel like failures. How should we respond on days that we miss the mark?

For starters, we should extend to ourselves the same grace God extends to us. As Paul declares, "...But where sin abounded, grace abounded much more" (Romans 5:20b). Of course, this is not a license to live as we please, but it is an assurance of the forgiving grace of God.

Also remember, life is a journey. We won't perfectly exemplify all of these characteristics at once. We are constantly learning, growing, and being refined by God's grace, through both crisis and everyday life. Trust in God's promise that "...He who has begun a good work in you will complete it until the day of Jesus Christ" (Philippians 1:6).

Let us commit to doing better tomorrow by the grace of God. He has promised us that failure is not final for the believer—"For a righteous man may fall seven times and rise again..." (Proverbs 24:16).

Each day is a new opportunity to restart and move forward in our walk with God. We should not let the Enemy whisper words of defeat and hopelessness. Let us choose, by God's grace, to move closer to Him than we were yesterday.

So, if we failed yesterday, we can choose to restart today.

Scriptures to Think On:

Who is a God like You, pardoning iniquity and passing over the transgression of the remnant of His heritage? He does not retain His anger forever, because He delights in mercy. He will again have compassion on us, and will subdue our iniquities. You will cast all our sins into the depths of the sea. **Micah 7:18-19**

Then He who sat on the throne said, "Behold, I make all things new." **Revelation 21:5**

JOURNAL

_____

_____

_____

_____

_____

_____

_____

_____

_____

_____

_____

_____

_____

_____

CONCLUSION

At the start of the COVID-19 crisis, one of my good friends and mentors asked me, "What do you want people to say about you when this crisis is over?" Those simple words became the north star for us throughout the crisis. Repeatedly, we asked ourselves:

- What will our loved ones say about us when all this is over?
- What will our church family say about us?
- What will our neighbors and coworkers say about us?
- What will the lost world say about us?
- Will people say that we lived out what we proclaimed all our lives?
- Will they say that we proved to be phonies?

Ultimately, what will God say about us? Will he say to us, "Well done, good and faithful servant; you have been faithful over a few things, I will make you ruler over many things. Enter into the joy of your lord." (Matthew 25:23), or will He call us, "You wicked and lazy servant" (Matthew 25:26)?

May it be said of each of us readers who confesses the name of Christ that throughout our crisis, our actions matched our confession.

ABOUT THE AUTHORS

Dr. Abidan Shah (PhD, Southeastern Baptist Theological Seminary) is the lead pastor of Clearview Church in Henderson, NC and professor of New Testament and Greek. He also serves as a chaplain to the local hospital, police department, and fire department. For more information, visit abidanshah.com.

Nicole Shah (Christian Counseling major, Toccoa Falls College, graduating in 2020) is active in ministry alongside her husband. The Shahs have four children and have been in ministry for over 20 years. For more information, visit clearviewbc.org.

Made in the USA
Middletown, DE
07 June 2020

97026646R00061